Welcom

Thank you for choosing this book. I hope you enjoy every moment with it. As token of my appreciation, I would like to offer you special gift.

Send a message for email oliviacarttman@gmail.com , you get special gift for FREE.

Scan the QR Code below to explore different High Contrast Books for your babies on every occasion.

ABOUT BOOK

Welcome to My First Advent Calendar High Contrast Baby Book – a magical introduction to the holiday season for your little one. Inside you'll find 25 enchanting black and white images of Christmas and winter elements, specially designed to stimulate your baby's visual development. Share your love for the festive season with your newborn as you explore each page, fostering the joy and wonder of Christmas from the very beginning. Start your baby's journey into the magical world of Christmas today!

THIS BOOK
BELONG TO:

Look at the shining stars in the night sky. Let's count them together: one, two.
Stars help us feel calm and safe, just like when we cuddle together.

Listen to the soft jingle of the bells. Ding, ding, ding! Can you hear them?
They make a happy sound, just like when we laugh together.

The soft glow of the candles brings warmth and light.
Can you feel the warmth in the air?
Just like a cozy blanket on a cold day.

A cheerful snowman stands tall in the snow. His round belly and big smile make him look so happy.
Imagine how cold the snow feels, but the snowman stays warm with his cozy scarf.

A friendly reindeer trots
through the snow with his
antlers held high.
His strong legs help him run
fast, and his soft fur keeps him
warm on chilly nights.

A bright stocking hangs by the fireplace, waiting to be filled with treats.
It sways gently, like it's ready for something special to arrive.

Colorful, shiny balls hang on the Christmas tree, reflecting the lights around them.
They sparkle like tiny stars, making everything feel magical.

The Christmas tree stands tall, its branches full of decorations. The smell of pine makes the air fresh and crisp, while its twinkling lights fill the room with joy.

Wrapped presents sit under the tree, each one tied with a colorful ribbon.

They are waiting patiently to be opened, holding surprises inside that bring joy and smiles.

A candy cane with red and white stripes twirls like a playful ribbon.
Its sweet taste makes everything feel merry and bright.

A peaceful angel with soft wings floats gently above, watching over with love and kindness. Her wings move like a soft breeze, bringing calm and peace.

12

A beautiful wreath made of green branches and red berries hangs proudly on the door. Its round shape welcomes everyone with warmth and happiness.

A playful elf with a bright hat
and pointy shoes dances around.
He's busy helping Santa,
spreading joy and laughter
everywhere he goes.

14

A gingerbread man with a big smile and buttons made of candy stands ready to bring cheer.
His sweet scent fills the air, making everything feel cozy and fun.

Santa Claus, with his kind smile, carries a big sack filled with presents.
He is ready to bring happiness to all the children.

A gingerbread house stands with candy decorations and frosting on the roof.
It smells sweet and looks cozy, like a tiny house full of holiday magic.

A playful penguin waddles through the snow, flapping his wings.
He's full of energy, sliding and hopping, ready for a winter adventure.

A fluffy polar bear walks slowly
across the icy snow.
His thick fur keeps him warm,
and he looks calm and peaceful
in the cold winter air.

A heart, full of love and
warmth, reminds us of the
kindness we share.
It glows softly, bringing a
feeling of comfort and joy.

A sled carries a big sack full of gifts, ready to bring joy to everyone.
It glides through the snow, filled with surprises waiting to be shared.

A pile of sweet treats, full of colorful candies and chocolates, is ready to bring smiles.
Each one is a little bite of happiness.

Soft, warm gloves keep our
hands cozy in the cold winter
air.
They fit snugly, ready to help
us explore snowy adventures.

A warm mug of hot chocolate, topped with fluffy marshmallows, makes the cold winter day feel cozy.
Each sip is sweet and comforting, like a warm hug.

The Holy Family sits peacefully together - Mary, Joseph, and baby Jesus.
Their love and care for each other fill the world with peace and hope.

A peaceful dove carries an olive
branch in its beak, a symbol of
hope and harmony.
Its gentle flight reminds us that
peace is always possible.

"Thank you for your purchase! My name is Olivia, and my interest in education and passion for creating for the youngest inspired me to write high contrast books.

If this book added value to your parenting journey or brought joy to your baby, I would be deeply grateful if you could spare a moment to leave a review. Your feedback helps other parents find the right books for their children.

Your review will help my book to stand out amongst the big publishing companies. Thank you so much for your support and for being a part of my self-publishing journey."

Made in the USA
Las Vegas, NV
10 December 2024

13782464R00031